I0490409

# Clocking Your Way to Triumph

Unlock the Time Management Secrets
of Successful Entrepreneurs

# Preface

Dear Time Conqueror,

As you hold this book in your hands, take a moment to ponder the significance of time in your life. Have you ever felt that there are never enough hours in a day to achieve all that you desire? Do you find yourself overwhelmed by endless tasks and responsibilities, constantly struggling to catch up with the fast-paced world of entrepreneurship?

If so, you are not alone. Countless entrepreneurs face similar challenges, battling the relentless ticking of the clock as they strive for success. But what if I told you that there is a way to harness the power of time, to bend it to your will and transform it into the ultimate ally for your business endeavors?

"Clocking Your Way to Triumph: Unlock the Time Management Secrets of Successful Entrepreneurs" is your guide to mastering the elusive art of time management, enabling you to achieve your entrepreneurial dreams and live a fulfilling, balanced life. This book is designed to equip you with the knowledge and skills necessary to overcome obstacles, boost productivity, and emerge victorious in your journey towards business success.

Ask yourself: Are you ready to embark on this transformative journey and unlock the true potential of your time? Are you willing to challenge old habits, adopt new strategies, and embrace the mindset of a time management master?

As you delve into the pages that follow, you will discover a treasure trove of practical tips, powerful strategies, and inspiring insights to help you overcome the challenges of time management. You will learn how to prioritize your tasks, set SMART goals, develop effective routines, and delegate with confidence. You will explore the science of procrastination, the power of networking, and the importance of mindfulness in your quest for success.

Each chapter is carefully crafted to provide actionable advice and motivation, ensuring that you not only read about these techniques but also apply them in your daily life. The case studies from successful entrepreneurs will serve as guiding stars, illuminating your path towards time management mastery.

As you stand on the threshold of a new chapter in your entrepreneurial journey, remember that time is both your greatest asset and your most formidable adversary. The choice is yours: Will you succumb to the pressures of time, or will you rise above them and seize control of your destiny?

Now, let us begin our journey into the world of time management, where every second counts and the triumph of your dreams awaits.

Yours in the pursuit of success,

Aditya

# Table Of Contents

# Chapter 1 - The Time Management Mindset: Embracing a Productive Entrepreneurial Lifestyle

As an entrepreneur, time is our most valuable resource. It's the one thing that, once spent, we can never get back. And in the world of entrepreneurship, where our success hinges on our ability to make the most of every opportunity, how we manage our time can make all the difference. In this chapter, I will take you on a journey to transform your mindset and embrace the power of effective time management. Together, we will unlock the secrets of a productive entrepreneurial lifestyle.

To start, let's reflect on a fundamental question: What does it mean to have a time management mindset? Is it simply about being more organized, or is there something deeper at play? The truth is, having a time management mindset means embracing a way of life that values time as the precious, non-renewable resource it is. It involves setting clear goals, ruthlessly prioritizing tasks, and constantly seeking ways to work smarter, not harder. This mindset drives us to make conscious choices about how we spend our time, and ultimately, how we shape our lives.

One of the key concepts in time management is the idea of "time ownership." This means taking full responsibility for how we spend our time and being accountable for the choices we make. Time ownership empowers us to recognize that we have control over our schedules and the ability to make meaningful changes. As entrepreneurs, it's crucial to own our time, to make sure we're directing our energy towards the tasks and activities that truly matter.

Now, let's consider the role of discipline in our time management journey. Discipline is the cornerstone of a

MR. ADITYA DHAR DUBEY

productive entrepreneurial lifestyle. It's the ability to stay focused on our goals, even when faced with distractions or setbacks. By cultivating discipline, we develop the mental fortitude to consistently choose the path that leads us closer to success. Ask yourself: How can I strengthen my discipline to make better use of my time?

As we dive deeper into our time management exploration, we must also examine our relationship with distractions. In today's fast-paced world, distractions are everywhere, and they can quickly derail our best-laid plans. The key is to develop strategies for identifying, minimizing, and overcoming distractions, so we can stay focused on what truly matters. What are the distractions that you encounter most frequently? How can you better manage them to protect your valuable time?

An essential component of the time management mindset is the practice of continuous improvement. This means constantly seeking ways to refine our processes, enhance our efficiency, and streamline our workflows. It's the willingness to learn from our mistakes, evaluate our progress, and adjust our strategies as needed. By embracing continuous improvement, we ensure that our time management skills grow and evolve alongside our businesses. What areas of your time management practices can you improve? What steps can you take to make those improvements a reality?

Finally, let's talk about the importance of balance. While we all strive for success in our entrepreneurial endeavors, it's crucial not to lose sight of the other aspects of our lives that bring us joy and fulfillment. By practicing effective time management, we can achieve a harmonious balance between our professional and personal lives, ensuring that we're not just successful entrepreneurs, but well-rounded individuals. How can you use time management to create a more balanced, fulfilling life?

In conclusion, the time management mindset is the foundation upon which we build our productive entrepreneurial lifestyle. By embracing this mindset, we take control of our time, own our choices, and create the life we've always dreamed of. As we move forward in this book, we'll explore specific strategies, techniques, and tools to help you master time management and unlock your full entrepreneurial potential. The journey has just begun. Let's make every moment count.

# Chapter 2 - Time Auditing: Identifying Your Time-Wasting Habits and Eliminating Them

In the previous chapter, we discussed the importance of embracing a time management mindset to lay the foundation for a productive entrepreneurial lifestyle. Now, it's time to take action and embark on our first essential step towards better time management: conducting a time audit.

A time audit is a systematic review of how you spend your time, aimed at identifying patterns and habits that hinder your productivity. By uncovering these time-wasting behaviors, you can develop targeted strategies to eliminate them, making way for increased efficiency and focus. In this chapter, I will guide you through the process of conducting a thorough time audit, and together, we will pave the way towards greater productivity and success.

### Step 1: Track your time

The first step in conducting a time audit is to track your time for at least one week. By doing so, you'll gain a clear understanding of how you currently allocate your hours and minutes. To track your time, you can use a pen and paper, a spreadsheet, or a time-tracking app, whichever method works best for you.

As you track your time, be sure to include every activity, no matter how small or insignificant it may seem. This includes work tasks, breaks, personal errands, and even time spent on social media or watching TV. The more detailed and accurate your records, the more valuable insights you'll gain from your time audit.

### Step 2: Analyze your data

Once you've tracked your time for a week, it's time to analyze the data. Look for patterns and trends in your time usage. Are there activities that take up a disproportionate amount of your time? Are there specific times of day when you're more or less productive? Are you spending more time on low-priority tasks than high-priority ones?

As you analyze your data, consider the following questions:

- Which tasks are consuming the majority of your time?
- Are there any activities that you could delegate or outsource?
- Are there recurring distractions that interrupt your workflow?
- Are you allocating enough time for strategic planning and long-term goals?

Step 3: Identify time-wasting habits

Now that you've analyzed your data, it's time to pinpoint the specific habits and behaviors that are wasting your precious time. These might include checking emails too frequently, spending excessive time on social media, or engaging in multitasking, which can hinder productivity.

To identify these time-wasting habits, ask yourself:

- What activities do I spend time on that don't contribute to my goals?
- Are there tasks I perform regularly that could be done more efficiently or eliminated altogether?
- Do I tend to procrastinate on certain tasks, and if so, why?

**Step 4: Develop targeted strategies**

With your time-wasting habits identified, you can now develop targeted strategies to eliminate them. For example, if you find that you're spending too much time on email, you might consider setting specific times throughout the day to check and respond to messages. If social media is a constant distraction, you could use an app to block access during designated work hours.

Remember, the goal is not to eliminate every non-work-related activity from your life, but rather to find a balance that allows you to be both productive and fulfilled. Consider the following questions as you develop your strategies:

- What boundaries can I set to minimize distractions and stay focused on my priorities?
- How can I leverage technology or tools to streamline my workflow and save time?
- What new habits can I develop to replace the time-wasting behaviors I've identified?

**Step 5: Implement and reassess**

With your strategies in place, it's time to implement them and monitor your progress. Be patient with yourself as you adjust to new habits and routines, and remember that change takes time. As you implement your new strategies, track your time once again to measure the impact of your changes. This will help you identify areas where you've made progress, as well as those that may require further adjustment.

After a few weeks of implementing your new strategies, reassess your time management practices. Ask yourself:

- Have my time-wasting habits decreased?
- Am I spending more time on high-priority tasks and goals?
- Have my productivity and focus improved?

If you find that some of your strategies aren't working as well as you'd hoped, don't be discouraged. Time management is an ongoing process, and it may take several iterations of your time audit to find the strategies that work best for you.

In conclusion, conducting a time audit is an invaluable tool for identifying time-wasting habits and developing targeted strategies to eliminate them. By taking control of your time and focusing on what truly matters, you'll be well on your way to unlocking your full entrepreneurial potential. In the next chapter, we will delve deeper into the art of prioritization, ensuring that you dedicate your valuable time to the tasks and activities that drive your success. The journey continues, and with each step, we grow closer to triumph.

# Chapter 3 - Prioritization Mastery: Deciding What Matters Most in Your Entrepreneurial Journey

In the previous chapters, we explored the time management mindset and learned how to conduct a time audit to identify and eliminate time-wasting habits. With these foundations in place, we can now turn our attention to mastering the art of prioritization, a critical skill for any successful entrepreneur.

Prioritization is the process of determining which tasks and activities are most important and allocating our time and resources accordingly. By mastering prioritization, we can focus our efforts on high-impact tasks, ensuring that we make meaningful progress towards our goals. In this chapter, I'll guide you through the process of prioritization mastery, providing actionable insights and strategies to help you make the most of your time.

**Step 1: Define your goals and objectives**

To prioritize effectively, we must first have a clear understanding of our goals and objectives. These provide the compass that guides our decision-making and helps us determine which tasks are truly important. Take some time to reflect on your long-term and short-term goals, both for your business and your personal life. Consider the following questions:

- What do I want to achieve in the next year, five years, and ten years?
- What milestones must I reach to accomplish these goals?
- Which objectives are most important for my business's growth and success?

## Step 2: Break down your goals into tasks

Once you've defined your goals and objectives, break them down into smaller, manageable tasks. This will help you identify the specific actions you need to take to make progress towards your goals. Create a list of tasks for each goal, and determine the approximate time and resources required to complete each one.

## Step 3: Categorize your tasks

Now that you have a list of tasks, it's time to categorize them based on their importance and urgency. A simple way to do this is by using the Eisenhower Matrix, which we'll explore in more depth in a later chapter. For now, categorize your tasks into one of the following four quadrants:

1. Important and urgent
2. Important but not urgent
3. Not important but urgent
4. Not important and not urgent

This categorization will help you visualize which tasks require your immediate attention and which can be scheduled for later or delegated.

## Step 4: Prioritize your tasks

With your tasks categorized, you can now prioritize them within each quadrant. Start by ranking the tasks in the "Important and urgent" quadrant, followed by those in the "Important but not urgent" quadrant. As you prioritize your tasks, consider factors such as deadlines, dependencies, and potential impact on your goals.

Remember, the goal of prioritization is not to complete every task on your list but to focus on the tasks that will have the most significant impact on your success.

## Step 5: Schedule your tasks

Now that you have a prioritized list of tasks, it's time to schedule them into your calendar. Start by allocating time for your most important and urgent tasks, ensuring that you have enough time to complete them before their deadlines. Then, schedule the important but not urgent tasks, taking care to balance your workload and avoid overcommitting.

As you schedule your tasks, consider the following questions:

- What is the most effective order for completing these tasks?

- Are there any dependencies between tasks that I need to account for?

- How can I ensure that I maintain a healthy work-life balance while pursuing my goals?

**Step 6: Review and adjust**

Finally, remember that prioritization is an ongoing process. Regularly review and adjust your priorities as new tasks emerge, deadlines change, or your goals evolve. This will help you stay focused on what truly matters and ensure that you continue to make meaningful progress towards your entrepreneurial success.

# Chapter 4 - The Power of Goal-Setting: Crafting SMART Goals to Drive Business Success

Now that we have explored the time management mindset, conducted a time audit, and mastered prioritization, it's time to focus on one of the most critical aspects of achieving entrepreneurial success: goal-setting. The goals we set for ourselves and our businesses play a vital role in guiding our actions and determining the direction of our growth. In this chapter, I will introduce you to the concept of SMART goals and provide actionable strategies for crafting goals that will propel you and your business towards success.

SMART is an acronym that stands for Specific, Measurable, Achievable, Relevant, and Time-bound. By crafting goals that meet these criteria, we can create a clear roadmap for our success, ensuring that we stay focused, motivated, and on track to achieve our objectives.

**Step 1: Make your goals Specific**

The first step in crafting SMART goals is to ensure that they are Specific. Specific goals provide a clear and unambiguous description of what you want to achieve, making it easier to plan the necessary steps and track your progress.

To create Specific goals, consider the following questions:

- What exactly do I want to achieve?
- Who is involved in achieving this goal?
- Where will the goal be accomplished?
- Why is this goal important to me and my business?

**Step 2: Ensure your goals are Measurable**

Measurable goals are those that have quantifiable outcomes, allowing you to track your progress and determine when the goal has been achieved. By setting Measurable goals, you can stay motivated by celebrating your progress along the way.

To make your goals Measurable, ask yourself:

- How will I know when I have achieved this goal?
- What metrics or indicators can I use to track my progress?

### Step 3: Set Achievable goals

Achievable goals strike the balance between being challenging and realistic. While it's essential to set goals that push you to grow and develop, they should also be within the realm of possibility given your current resources, skills, and constraints.

To ensure your goals are Achievable, consider:

- Do I have the resources and skills needed to achieve this goal, or can I acquire them?
- Are there any external factors or constraints that may impact my ability to achieve this goal?

### Step 4: Keep your goals Relevant

Relevant goals align with your broader business objectives and contribute to your long-term success. By setting goals that are Relevant, you can ensure that your efforts are focused on the tasks and activities that truly matter.

To determine if a goal is Relevant, ask yourself:

- Does this goal align with my overall business objectives and values?
- Will achieving this goal contribute to my long-term success?

### Step 5: Set Time-bound goals

Finally, SMART goals are Time-bound, meaning they have a clear deadline or timeframe for completion. By setting Time-bound goals, you create a sense of urgency that helps you stay focused and motivated to achieve your objectives.

To make your goals Time-bound, consider:

- What is a realistic timeframe for achieving this goal?
- Are there any milestones or interim deadlines that I should set to track my progress?

By following these steps and crafting SMART goals, you will create a clear and actionable roadmap for your entrepreneurial success. As you work towards your goals, remember to stay flexible and adapt your plans as needed. Regularly review your goals and adjust them as your business grows, your priorities shift, or new opportunities arise.

In the next chapter, we'll delve into the Eisenhower Matrix, a powerful tool for strategically sorting your tasks and maximizing efficiency. With your SMART goals in place and a solid foundation in time management, you'll be well-equipped to tackle the challenges and seize the opportunities that lie ahead.

# Chapter 5 - The Eisenhower Matrix: Strategically Sorting Your Tasks for Maximum Efficiency

So far, we've explored the time management mindset, conducted a time audit, mastered prioritization, and learned the power of goal-setting. With this foundation in place, we can now turn our attention to a practical tool that will help you make even better use of your time: the Eisenhower Matrix. In this chapter, I will guide you through the process of using the Eisenhower Matrix to sort your tasks and maximize your efficiency, ensuring that you remain focused on your most important and urgent tasks.

The Eisenhower Matrix, also known as the Urgent-Important Matrix, is a time management tool that helps you prioritize tasks based on their urgency and importance. It was popularized by President Dwight D. Eisenhower, who was known for his ability to make difficult decisions and manage his time effectively. The matrix consists of four quadrants, each representing a different combination of urgency and importance:

1. Important and Urgent
2. Important but Not Urgent
3. Not Important but Urgent
4. Not Important and Not Urgent

By sorting your tasks into these quadrants, you can gain a clearer understanding of where to focus your time and energy.

**Step 1: List your tasks**

Begin by creating a list of all the tasks you need to complete. This should include tasks related to your work, personal life, and long-term goals. Be as comprehensive as possible, including both large and small tasks.

**Step 2: Assign importance and urgency**

Next, evaluate each task on your list based on its importance and urgency. Importance refers to the significance of a task in terms of its alignment with your goals and values, while urgency refers to the timeframe within which a task must be completed.

To assign importance and urgency, ask yourself the following questions:

- Does this task contribute significantly to my long-term goals and objectives?
- Is there a deadline or external pressure associated with this task?

**Step 3: Sort tasks into the matrix**

With each task assigned an importance and urgency rating, you can now sort them into the appropriate quadrant of the Eisenhower Matrix. Place each task in one of the four quadrants based on its assigned ratings:

1. Important and Urgent: Tasks that are both important and require immediate attention.
2. Important but Not Urgent: Tasks that are important but can be scheduled for later.
3. Not Important but Urgent: Tasks that require immediate attention but are not crucial to your long-term goals.
4. Not Important and Not Urgent: Tasks that are neither important nor urgent and should be either delegated, eliminated, or scheduled for a later time when other priorities have been addressed.

**Step 4: Plan your actions**

With your tasks sorted into the Eisenhower Matrix, you can now plan your actions accordingly. Here's a suggested approach for each quadrant:

1. Important and Urgent: Tackle these tasks first, ensuring

that you allocate enough time and resources to complete them on time.

2. Important but Not Urgent: Schedule these tasks for completion after the important and urgent tasks, but before the not important but urgent tasks. These tasks often contribute most to your long-term success, so be sure to allocate regular time to work on them.

3. Not Important but Urgent: If possible, delegate these tasks to someone else or find ways to streamline their completion. If you must complete them yourself, do so after addressing the tasks in quadrants 1 and 2.

4. Not Important and Not Urgent: Consider eliminating these tasks or scheduling them for a time when you have completed higher-priority tasks.

By following these steps and using the Eisenhower Matrix, you will be better equipped to manage your time effectively and focus on the tasks that truly matter. In the next chapter, we will explore the Pomodoro Technique, a powerful method for boosting focus and reducing burnout through structured work sessions. Combined with the insights you've gained from the Eisenhower Matrix, this technique will further enhance your time management skills and help you make even greater strides towards your entrepreneurial success. Keep in mind that, as with all time management strategies, it's essential to adapt the Eisenhower Matrix to your unique circumstances and priorities, ensuring that it serves you well on your journey to triumph.

# Chapter 6 - The Pomodoro Technique: Boosting Focus and Reducing Burnout Through Structured Work Sessions

With a solid foundation in the time management mindset, time auditing, prioritization, goal-setting, and the Eisenhower Matrix, we are now ready to explore another powerful tool to help you manage your time more effectively: the Pomodoro Technique. In this chapter, I will introduce you to the Pomodoro Technique and provide actionable steps for implementing this approach in your daily work routine. By using this method, you can boost your focus, reduce burnout, and make the most of the time you have available.

The Pomodoro Technique, developed by Francesco Cirillo in the late 1980s, is a time management method based on the idea of breaking work into short, focused intervals (called "Pomodoros") separated by brief breaks. This approach helps to maintain concentration and prevent burnout by providing regular mental rest periods.

Here's how to implement the Pomodoro Technique:

**Step 1: Choose a task**

Identify a task you want to work on, preferably one that requires deep focus and attention. This task could be related to your work, personal life, or long-term goals.

**Step 2: Set a timer for 25 minutes**

Using a timer (either a physical one or an app on your phone), set a countdown for 25 minutes. This duration is the length of a standard Pomodoro.

**Step 3: Work on the task**

Begin working on your chosen task with full concentration,

aiming to make as much progress as possible during the 25-minute interval. If you find your mind wandering or distractions arising, gently bring your focus back to the task at hand.

## Step 4: Take a short break

When the timer goes off, take a 5-minute break. Use this time to rest your mind and recharge your mental energy. You could stretch, walk around, or engage in a brief, non-work-related activity.

## Step 5: Repeat the process

After your short break, return to your task and set the timer for another 25-minute Pomodoro. Continue working through your task in these focused intervals, taking a 5-minute break after each Pomodoro.

## Step 6: Take a longer break

After completing four Pomodoros, take a longer break of 15 to 30 minutes. This extended break will help to prevent burnout and maintain your productivity throughout the day.

As you begin implementing the Pomodoro Technique, consider the following questions:

- How does breaking my work into shorter intervals affect my focus and productivity?

- What adjustments can I make to the Pomodoro Technique to better suit my unique work style and preferences?

- How can I apply the principles of the Pomodoro Technique to other aspects of my life, such as personal projects or daily routines?

In the next chapter, we will explore the concept of time blocking, a complementary approach to scheduling your day for optimal productivity and work-life balance. By combining the Pomodoro Technique with time blocking and the other time management strategies we've discussed so far, you will be well-equipped to make the most of your time and achieve your entrepreneurial goals.

# Chapter 7 - Time Blocking: Scheduling Your Day for Optimal Productivity and Work-Life Balance

As we continue our journey to unlock the time management secrets of successful entrepreneurs, we now turn our attention to time blocking, a powerful technique for organizing your day and maximizing productivity. By combining the principles of time blocking with the techniques we've already discussed, such as the Pomodoro Technique and the Eisenhower Matrix, you can create a holistic time management system that supports both your professional and personal goals. In this chapter, I will guide you through the process of implementing time blocking in your daily routine, ensuring that you make the most of every hour and strike the perfect work-life balance.

Time blocking involves dividing your day into designated blocks of time, with each block dedicated to a specific task or group of tasks. This approach enables you to concentrate on one thing at a time, reduces the impact of distractions, and helps ensure that your most important tasks receive the attention they deserve.

Here's how to implement time blocking in your daily schedule:

**Step 1: Identify your priorities**

Review your goals, projects, and tasks, and determine which are the most important and time-sensitive. Use the insights you've gained from the Eisenhower Matrix to help you prioritize your tasks effectively.

**Step 2: Estimate the time required**

For each of your priority tasks, estimate how much time you will need to complete them. Be realistic, but also account for the possibility of unforeseen obstacles or delays.

## Step 3: Create time blocks

Divide your day into blocks of time, ranging from 30 minutes to several hours, depending on the nature of the tasks you're planning to tackle. As you create your time blocks, keep the following tips in mind:

- Schedule your most important and demanding tasks during your peak energy and focus periods, typically in the morning or early afternoon.

- Allow for breaks and transition time between tasks, giving yourself space to rest and mentally prepare for the next task.

- Include time for personal activities, such as exercise, hobbies, and socializing, to ensure a healthy work-life balance.

## Step 4: Assign tasks to time blocks

Allocate your tasks to the appropriate time blocks, taking into account your energy levels, deadlines, and other commitments. Be realistic about how much you can accomplish in a given block, and avoid overloading your schedule.

## Step 5: Monitor your progress and adjust as needed

As you implement time blocking, track your progress and note any challenges or inefficiencies that arise. Use this information to refine your approach and make adjustments to your time blocks as needed.

Consider these thought-provoking questions as you implement time blocking:

- How does time blocking affect my productivity and focus throughout the day?

- What adjustments can I make to my time blocks to better align with my natural energy patterns and work preferences?

- How can I use time blocking to create a healthier work-life balance?

In the next chapter, we will explore the art of delegation, a crucial skill for leveraging your team to achieve more in less time. By mastering time blocking and learning to delegate effectively, you will be well on your way to unlocking the full potential of your time and achieving the triumph you seek.

# Chapter 8 - The Art of Delegation: Leveraging Your Team to Achieve More in Less Time

As you continue to refine your time management skills, it's essential to recognize that you cannot do everything yourself. The art of delegation is a vital skill for entrepreneurs looking to scale their business and achieve long-term success. By delegating tasks to your team, you can free up your valuable time to focus on high-priority tasks and strategic decision-making. In this chapter, I will guide you through the process of effective delegation, providing actionable steps to help you leverage your team's strengths and achieve more in less time.

## Step 1: Identify tasks suitable for delegation

Review your list of tasks and projects, and determine which ones can be effectively delegated to others. Tasks suitable for delegation typically meet one or more of the following criteria:

- They are time-consuming but not strategically critical.
- They require skills or expertise that other team members possess.
- They are routine or repetitive in nature and do not require your personal attention.

## Step 2: Choose the right person for the task

Consider the skills, expertise, and workload of your team members when deciding whom to delegate tasks to. Match tasks with individuals who have the appropriate skillset and capacity to take them on, ensuring that the task aligns with their strengths and professional development goals.

## Step 3: Communicate clearly and set expectations

When delegating tasks, provide clear and concise instructions, outlining the desired outcome, deadline, and any relevant resources or guidelines. Set realistic expectations for the task, and ensure that the person you are delegating to has a thorough understanding of their responsibilities and any potential challenges they may encounter.

### Step 4: Provide support and resources

Ensure that your team members have the necessary resources and support to complete the tasks you've delegated to them. This may include training, access to information, or collaboration with other team members.

### Step 5: Monitor progress and provide feedback

Check in with your team members regularly to monitor their progress on delegated tasks and provide feedback, guidance, or assistance as needed. Keep lines of communication open and encourage them to ask questions or raise concerns if they encounter difficulties.

### Step 6: Recognize and reward success

Acknowledge the successful completion of delegated tasks and express your appreciation for your team members' efforts. Providing positive feedback and recognition can help motivate your team and build trust, making future delegation efforts more effective.

Consider these thought-provoking questions as you practice the art of delegation:

- How does delegating tasks to my team affect my ability to focus on high-priority tasks and strategic decision-making?

- What barriers or challenges do I face when delegating tasks, and how can I overcome them?

- How can I better leverage the strengths and expertise of my team members to achieve our collective goals?

In the next chapter, we will delve into the importance of routine, exploring how creating daily habits can contribute to sustainable success. By mastering delegation and implementing effective routines, you'll be well on your way to unlocking the time management secrets of successful entrepreneurs and achieving the triumph you seek.

# Chapter 9 - The Importance of Routine: Creating Daily Habits for Sustainable Success

As you continue to develop your time management skills, it's crucial to recognize the power of routine in achieving sustainable success. Establishing daily habits can help you maintain focus, increase productivity, and create a sense of stability in your entrepreneurial journey. In this chapter, I will provide actionable steps to help you develop routines that support your personal and professional goals, ensuring that you remain on the path to triumph.

**Step 1: Identify key habits for success**

Reflect on the tasks and activities that contribute most to your success and well-being, both personally and professionally. These might include regular exercise, healthy eating, dedicated time for strategic thinking, or daily progress on important projects. Create a list of the key habits you want to incorporate into your daily routine.

**Step 2: Set realistic goals for habit formation**

For each habit you've identified, set a realistic goal for how often you want to engage in the activity. Start small, focusing on consistency rather than intensity, and gradually increase the frequency or duration of the habit as you build momentum.

**Step 3: Schedule time for your habits**

Using the time blocking technique discussed in Chapter 7, allocate specific time slots in your daily schedule for your key habits. Prioritize these activities, treating them as non-negotiable commitments in your calendar.

**Step 4: Create triggers and cues for your habits**

Establish triggers or cues that signal it's time to engage in a specific habit. For example, you might choose to exercise immediately after waking up or dedicate the first hour of your workday to strategic thinking. By associating your habits with specific triggers or cues, you increase the likelihood of maintaining consistency.

**Step 5: Monitor your progress and adjust as needed**

Track your success in maintaining your daily habits and reflect on any challenges or obstacles that arise. Use this information to refine your approach, making adjustments to your schedule or habits as needed.

**Step 6: Celebrate your successes and maintain accountability**

Recognize your achievements in maintaining your daily habits and celebrate your progress toward your goals. Share your successes with friends, family, or colleagues to maintain accountability and stay motivated.

Consider these thought-provoking questions as you develop your daily routines:

- How do my daily habits contribute to my overall success and well-being?

- What challenges or obstacles do I face in maintaining consistency in my routines, and how can I overcome them?

- How can I create an environment that supports my daily habits and routines?

In the next chapter, we will explore the relationship between technology and time management, examining top tools and apps that can support your time management efforts. By mastering the power of routine and leveraging technology to your advantage, you will continue to unlock the secrets of successful entrepreneurs and achieve the triumph you desire.

# Chapter 10 - Technology and Time Management: Top Tools and Apps for Busy Entrepreneurs

As an entrepreneur, you're constantly juggling multiple tasks and responsibilities. With the right tools and apps, you can streamline your workflow, stay organized, and maximize your productivity. In this chapter, I will introduce you to some of the top technology solutions that can support your time management efforts and help you unlock the secrets of successful entrepreneurs. I will also provide actionable steps to help you effectively integrate these tools into your daily routine.

**Step 1: Assess your needs**

Before diving into the vast array of available tools and apps, take the time to assess your specific needs and priorities. Consider which aspects of your time management and productivity could benefit most from technological support, and focus on finding solutions that address these areas.

**Step 2: Research and select the right tools**

Based on your identified needs, research various tools and apps that cater to your requirements. Read reviews, explore features, and consider compatibility with your existing systems. Some popular categories of time management tools include:

- Task and project management: Tools like Trello, Asana, and Basecamp can help you organize and track tasks, manage deadlines, and collaborate with your team.

- Time tracking: Apps like Toggl, Harvest, and Clockify allow you to track the time spent on specific tasks or projects, providing valuable insights into your productivity and time allocation.

- Calendar and scheduling: Tools such as Google Calendar, Microsoft Outlook, and Calendly can help you manage your appointments, deadlines, and availability, as well as synchronize your schedule across devices.

- Communication and collaboration: Platforms like Slack, Microsoft Teams, and Zoom can facilitate efficient communication, file sharing, and collaboration among team members, whether you're working in the same office or remotely.

### Step 3: Implement and integrate the tools into your workflow

Once you've selected the tools that best meet your needs, integrate them into your daily routine. Dedicate time to learning how to use each tool effectively and customize the settings to fit your workflow. Encourage your team to adopt these tools and provide training or resources as needed.

### Step 4: Evaluate and refine your tech stack

Periodically review the effectiveness of the tools and apps you've implemented, assessing whether they are helping you achieve your time management and productivity goals. Be open to refining your tech stack, replacing or adding tools as needed to further optimize your workflow.

Consider these thought-provoking questions as you explore the role of technology in your time management efforts:

- How can technology support my time management goals and help me achieve greater productivity?

- What challenges or obstacles might I face in implementing new tools or apps, and how can I overcome them?

- How can I create a balanced approach to technology, ensuring that it enhances my productivity without creating unnecessary distractions or complexity?

In the next chapter, we will delve into the science of procrastination, examining its causes and strategies for overcoming this common challenge. By effectively leveraging technology and conquering procrastination, you'll be well on your way to mastering the time management secrets of successful entrepreneurs and achieving the triumph you seek.

# Chapter 11 - The Science of Procrastination: Understanding Its Causes and Overcoming It

Procrastination is a common challenge faced by entrepreneurs, often standing in the way of effective time management and ultimate success. By understanding the science behind procrastination and implementing actionable strategies to combat it, you can unlock your full potential and move closer to triumph in your entrepreneurial journey. In this chapter, I will help you explore the causes of procrastination and provide practical techniques to overcome this productivity barrier.

### Step 1: Identify the causes of your procrastination

Procrastination often arises from a variety of factors, including fear of failure, perfectionism, lack of motivation, or simply feeling overwhelmed by the task at hand. Reflect on your own tendencies to procrastinate, and identify the underlying causes that may be holding you back.

### Step 2: Break tasks into manageable chunks

One effective strategy to combat procrastination is to break large tasks into smaller, more manageable components. By doing so, you can reduce the sense of overwhelm and make it easier to get started on a project. Set mini-deadlines for each task to maintain momentum and stay on track.

### Step 3: Implement the two-minute rule

Popularized by productivity expert David Allen, the two-minute rule states that if a task takes less than two minutes to complete, you should do it immediately. This approach helps you tackle small tasks quickly and efficiently, preventing them from piling up and contributing to a sense of overwhelm.

Step 4: Prioritize and schedule your most important tasks

Using the prioritization techniques discussed earlier in this book, such as the Eisenhower Matrix and the 80/20 rule, identify your most important tasks and schedule dedicated time to work on them. By focusing on high-impact tasks, you can make significant progress even when procrastination strikes.

**Step 5: Create a supportive environment**

Design your workspace and daily routine to minimize distractions and support productivity. Establish routines that promote focus, such as the Pomodoro Technique, and eliminate unnecessary interruptions that can derail your progress.

**Step 6: Practice self-compassion**

Recognize that everyone experiences procrastination to some degree, and practice self-compassion when you find yourself falling into this trap. Rather than berating yourself for your perceived failures, focus on learning from your experiences and developing strategies to improve your time management and productivity moving forward.

Consider these thought-provoking questions as you work to overcome procrastination:

- What are the underlying causes of my procrastination, and how can I address them?

- How can I break down large tasks into smaller components to reduce the sense of overwhelm?

- What routines and environmental changes can I implement to support productivity and minimize procrastination?

In the next chapter, we will explore decision-making hacks to streamline your choices and save time and energy. By conquering procrastination and optimizing your decision-making processes, you'll be well on your way to mastering the time management secrets of successful entrepreneurs and achieving the triumph you seek.

# Chapter 12 - Decision-Making Hacks: Streamlining Your Choices to Save Time and Energy

As an entrepreneur, you're faced with countless decisions each day, ranging from the seemingly trivial to the critical. Effective decision-making is a crucial aspect of time management, and streamlining this process can help you save time, energy, and mental bandwidth. In this chapter, I will share actionable hacks to help you make efficient and well-informed decisions, moving you closer to your entrepreneurial triumph.

### Step 1: Develop a clear decision-making framework

Establishing a consistent decision-making framework allows you to quickly evaluate options and make informed choices. Consider factors such as your values, long-term goals, and priorities when developing your framework. Align your decisions with these guiding principles to ensure they support your overall vision and objectives.

### Step 2: Limit your options

Having too many options can lead to decision paralysis and wasted time. Limit your choices by setting criteria or boundaries for your decision-making process. By narrowing your focus, you'll be able to evaluate options more efficiently and come to a conclusion more quickly.

### Step 3: Implement the 10-10-10 rule

The 10-10-10 rule, coined by author Suzy Welch, encourages you to consider the implications of your decision in three different timeframes: 10 minutes, 10 months, and 10 years from now. This approach helps you assess both short- and long-term consequences, ensuring that your decisions align with your overarching goals and priorities.

## Step 4: Make use of decision-making tools and techniques

Leverage tools and techniques such as decision matrices, pros and cons lists, or the "Six Thinking Hats" method to facilitate structured decision-making. These methods can help you evaluate options more objectively and efficiently, leading to better outcomes and reduced decision-making time.

## Step 5: Trust your intuition

While analysis and logic play an essential role in decision-making, your intuition can also provide valuable insights. Learn to trust your gut feelings and instincts, particularly when faced with complex or ambiguous situations where complete information may not be available.

## Step 6: Embrace the "good enough" mindset

Perfectionism can be a significant obstacle to efficient decision-making. Recognize that, in many cases, a "good enough" decision is better than no decision at all. Be willing to accept some degree of uncertainty and risk, and avoid letting the pursuit of perfection paralyze your decision-making process.

Consider these thought-provoking questions as you work to optimize your decision-making:

- How does my current decision-making process align with my values, goals, and priorities?

- What tools and techniques can I use to evaluate options more efficiently and objectively?

- How can I balance logic and intuition in my decision-making to achieve the best possible outcomes?

In the next chapter, we will delve into the concept of mastering the 80/20 rule, focusing on high-impact tasks for maximum results. By refining your decision-making processes and honing your ability to identify and prioritize high-impact tasks, you'll be well on your way to mastering the time management secrets of successful entrepreneurs and achieving the triumph you seek.

# Chapter 13 - Mastering the 80/20 Rule: How to Focus on High-Impact Tasks for Maximum Results

The 80/20 rule, also known as the Pareto Principle, is a powerful concept that can revolutionize your time management and productivity. It states that 80% of your results come from just 20% of your efforts. By identifying and focusing on the high-impact tasks that drive the most significant results, you can achieve more with less effort. In this chapter, I will guide you through actionable steps to apply the 80/20 rule in your entrepreneurial journey, optimizing your time and energy for maximum results.

**Step 1: Analyze your tasks and activities**

Begin by listing all the tasks and activities you perform in your business. This comprehensive inventory will provide the foundation for your 80/20 analysis, allowing you to identify which tasks truly drive results.

**Step 2: Assess the impact of each task**

Evaluate each task on your list based on the impact it has on your business success. Consider factors such as revenue generation, customer satisfaction, and long-term growth. This process will help you determine which tasks contribute most significantly to your results.

**Step 3: Identify the 20% of high-impact tasks**

Using your impact assessment, identify the top 20% of tasks that generate the most significant results. These high-impact tasks are the ones you should prioritize and allocate your time and resources towards.

**Step 4: Optimize your time and resources**

With your high-impact tasks identified, allocate more time and resources to these tasks while reducing the time spent on low-impact activities. By focusing on the tasks that truly drive results, you can maximize your productivity and achieve more with less effort.

**Step 5: Continuously evaluate and adjust**

The 80/20 rule is not a one-time exercise. Regularly review your tasks and their impact, adjusting your focus as necessary to ensure you are consistently directing your efforts towards high-impact activities. This ongoing evaluation will help you maintain peak productivity and adapt to changing circumstances in your business.

Consider these thought-provoking questions as you work to apply the 80/20 rule:

- What tasks and activities have the most significant impact on my business success?

- How can I allocate more time and resources to high-impact tasks while reducing my focus on low-impact activities?

- How can I continuously evaluate and adjust my focus to maintain alignment with the 80/20 rule?

In the next chapter, we will explore the value of downtime, emphasizing the importance of rest and recovery for long-term entrepreneurial success. By mastering the 80/20 rule and embracing the necessity of downtime, you will be well-equipped to unlock the time management secrets of successful entrepreneurs and achieve the triumph you seek.

# Chapter 14 - The Value of Downtime: Rest and Recovery for Long-Term Entrepreneurial Success

In the pursuit of triumph, it's easy to get caught up in the hustle and overlook the value of downtime. However, rest and recovery are essential for sustainable success and optimal performance. In this chapter, I will provide actionable strategies for incorporating downtime into your busy entrepreneurial life, ensuring that you maintain the energy and mental clarity required for long-term achievement.

**Step 1: Recognize the importance of downtime**

Downtime plays a crucial role in maintaining your mental, emotional, and physical health. It allows you to recharge, process information, and enhance creativity. Acknowledging the value of downtime is the first step towards making it a priority in your life.

**Step 2: Schedule regular downtime**

To ensure that downtime becomes an integral part of your routine, schedule regular periods of rest and relaxation. This could include daily breaks, weekly days off, or extended vacations. Treat downtime as an essential commitment and prioritize it just as you would any other important task.

**Step 3: Set boundaries between work and personal life**

Establish clear boundaries between your work and personal life to prevent burnout and ensure adequate downtime. This might involve setting specific work hours, disconnecting from work-related communication during non-work hours, or designating a dedicated workspace separate from your personal space.

**Step 4: Engage in restorative activities**

Make the most of your downtime by engaging in activities that truly rejuvenate and restore you. This could include physical exercise, spending time with loved ones, pursuing hobbies, or practicing mindfulness and meditation. Choose activities that align with your interests and needs, and prioritize them during your downtime.

## Step 5: Learn to detach from work

Cultivate the ability to mentally and emotionally detach from work during your downtime. This may involve developing techniques to manage work-related stress and anxiety or practicing mindfulness to maintain a sense of presence and focus on the present moment.

Consider these thought-provoking questions as you work to prioritize downtime:

- What are the potential consequences of neglecting downtime in my entrepreneurial journey?
- How can I establish clear boundaries between my work and personal life to ensure adequate rest and recovery?
- What activities or practices help me feel rejuvenated and restored during my downtime?

In the next chapter, we will delve into time management strategies for remote work, adapting our techniques for the digital age. By balancing focused work with intentional downtime, you will be well-equipped to maintain long-term success and unlock the time management secrets of successful entrepreneurs.

# Chapter 15 - Time Management for Remote Work: Adapting Strategies for the Digital Age

Remote work has become increasingly prevalent in the entrepreneurial landscape, offering flexibility and convenience. However, managing time effectively in a remote setting can be challenging. In this chapter, I will provide actionable strategies for optimizing time management while working remotely, ensuring productivity and success in the digital age.

### Step 1: Establish a dedicated workspace

Create a dedicated workspace in your home or remote location to maintain focus and separate work from personal life. This designated area should be comfortable, free from distractions, and equipped with the necessary tools and resources to support your work.

### Step 2: Set a consistent schedule

Establish a consistent work schedule, including start and end times, breaks, and lunch hours. This structure will help you maintain a sense of routine and discipline, which is crucial for effective time management.

### Step 3: Prioritize tasks and set daily goals

Each day, prioritize your tasks based on importance and deadlines, setting clear and achievable goals for what you aim to accomplish. This will help you stay focused and productive throughout the day.

### Step 4: Utilize time management techniques

Incorporate time management techniques, such as the Pomodoro Technique, time blocking, or the Eisenhower Matrix, to stay organized and maintain productivity. Experiment with different methods to find the one that best suits your remote work style.

## Step 5: Limit distractions

Identify potential distractions in your remote work environment and take steps to minimize them. This may involve using noise-cancelling headphones, setting boundaries with family members, or utilizing tools and apps to block time-wasting websites.

## Step 6: Communicate effectively with your team

Maintain open and effective communication with your team, utilizing digital tools such as video conferencing, instant messaging, and project management software. This will help keep everyone on the same page and ensure smooth collaboration.

## Step 7: Take regular breaks

Schedule regular breaks throughout your workday to recharge and maintain focus. Use this time to stretch, take a walk, or engage in a brief, restorative activity.

Consider these thought-provoking questions as you work to optimize time management for remote work:

- How can I create a dedicated workspace that promotes focus and productivity?
- What potential distractions do I need to address in my remote work environment?
- How can I maintain effective communication with my team while working remotely?

In the next chapter, we will explore effective meeting strategies, maximizing time, and collaboration in business discussions. By mastering time management for remote work, you will be well-prepared to navigate the challenges of the digital age and continue your journey towards entrepreneurial triumph.

# Chapter 16 - Effective Meeting Strategies: Maximizing Time and Collaboration in Business Discussions

Meetings are a crucial aspect of entrepreneurship, fostering collaboration, decision-making, and innovation. However, poorly managed meetings can be time-consuming and unproductive. In this chapter, I will provide actionable strategies for conducting effective meetings that maximize time and collaboration, ultimately driving your business forward.

### Step 1: Set clear objectives

Before scheduling a meeting, establish clear objectives outlining the purpose, goals, and desired outcomes. This clarity will help participants understand the meeting's significance and come prepared to contribute effectively.

### Step 2: Invite the right participants

Only invite participants who are essential to the meeting's objectives, ensuring focused discussion and efficient use of time. Avoid overloading meetings with unnecessary attendees who may not directly contribute to the desired outcomes.

### Step 3: Create an agenda

Develop a detailed agenda that outlines the topics to be covered, the allotted time for each item, and the designated speakers or presenters. Distribute the agenda to all participants in advance, allowing them to prepare and ensuring a structured and efficient meeting.

### Step 4: Set time limits and adhere to them

Establish time limits for each agenda item and the overall meeting duration, and adhere to these limits. This will help maintain focus, prevent unnecessary tangents, and ensure that all critical topics are addressed.

## Step 5: Assign roles and responsibilities

Designate specific roles and responsibilities for the meeting, such as a facilitator, note-taker, and timekeeper. These individuals will help keep the meeting on track, ensure that all voices are heard, and capture key takeaways for future reference.

## Step 6: Encourage active participation

Promote a collaborative and inclusive environment by encouraging all participants to contribute their thoughts, ideas, and feedback. Utilize techniques such as round-robin discussions, brainstorming sessions, or breakout groups to engage all attendees and foster open communication.

## Step 7: Follow up with action items

After the meeting, distribute a summary of key takeaways, decisions, and action items, including responsible parties and deadlines. This follow-up will ensure accountability and help maintain momentum towards achieving the meeting's objectives.

Consider these thought-provoking questions as you work to optimize your meeting strategies:

- How can I improve the structure and efficiency of my current meetings?

- What techniques can I employ to foster active participation and collaboration in my meetings?

- How can I ensure that meeting outcomes are translated into actionable steps and progress?

In the next chapter, we will delve into the power of networking and building relationships while effectively managing your time. By implementing effective meeting strategies, you will maximize collaboration, make better use of your time, and propel your entrepreneurial journey towards triumph.

# Chapter 17 - The Power of Networking: Building Relationships While Managing Your Time

Networking is a crucial aspect of entrepreneurship, providing opportunities to forge connections, learn from others, and potentially gain access to resources and partnerships. In this chapter, we will explore how to effectively build relationships through networking while managing your time efficiently.

**Step 1: Set clear networking objectives**

Before attending a networking event or engaging in networking activities, define your objectives. Ask yourself:

- What do I hope to achieve through networking?
- What types of connections am I seeking?
- How can networking benefit my business and personal growth?

By setting clear objectives, you can focus your networking efforts on activities that align with your goals.

**Step 2: Choose the right networking events**

Research and select networking events that align with your objectives and target audience. Attending relevant events will maximize your chances of connecting with like-minded individuals and forming meaningful relationships.

**Step 3: Prepare an elevator pitch**

Develop a concise, engaging elevator pitch that summarizes your business and personal brand. This pitch will allow you to quickly and effectively introduce yourself and your business, leaving a lasting impression on new connections.

## Step 4: Master the art of active listening

Effective networking is not just about speaking; it's about listening. Practice active listening by giving your full attention to the person you are speaking with, asking open-ended questions, and genuinely engaging with their ideas and perspectives.

## Step 5: Follow up and nurture connections

After a networking event, follow up with your new connections through personalized messages or emails, expressing your gratitude for the conversation and interest in staying connected. Nurture these relationships over time by regularly engaging with your contacts and providing value through insights, resources, or collaboration opportunities.

## Step 6: Leverage technology for efficient networking

Utilize technology and online platforms to network more efficiently. LinkedIn, for example, can help you connect with professionals in your industry and discover relevant networking events. Social media can also help you engage with your connections and share valuable content that showcases your expertise.

Consider these thought-provoking questions as you work on your networking strategy:

- How can I enhance my networking skills to build stronger connections?
- How can I identify networking opportunities that align with my objectives?
- How can I utilize technology to maximize my networking efforts while managing my time effectively?

In the next chapter, we will discuss the art of saying "no" and how to protect your time and priorities from unnecessary distractions. By leveraging the power of networking, you can build relationships that support your entrepreneurial journey while effectively managing your time.

# Chapter 18 - The Art of Saying "No": Protecting Your Time and Priorities from Unnecessary Distractions

As an entrepreneur, you'll encounter many opportunities and requests for your time and attention. While some of these may be beneficial, others can become distractions that hinder your progress. In this chapter, we will explore the art of saying "no" to protect your time and priorities from unnecessary distractions.

**Step 1: Evaluate the opportunity or request**

When faced with an opportunity or request, take a moment to assess its value and alignment with your goals. Ask yourself:

- How does this opportunity or request align with my priorities and objectives?
- What will be the time commitment, and is it worth the potential benefits?

**Step 2: Determine your response**

If the opportunity or request doesn't align with your priorities or objectives, it's important to say "no" respectfully and assertively. Keep in mind that saying "no" doesn't mean you're being selfish or unhelpful; it's about protecting your time and ensuring you can focus on what's truly important.

**Step 3: Communicate your decision**

When saying "no," be clear, concise, and respectful. Express your gratitude for the opportunity or request, and then explain your decision without over-justifying. For example:

"Thank you for thinking of me for this project. I appreciate the opportunity, but unfortunately, I cannot commit to it at this time, as I'm focusing on my current priorities."

## Step 4: Offer alternatives or suggestions

If possible, provide alternative solutions or suggestions to help the requester achieve their goals without your direct involvement. This can help maintain positive relationships while still protecting your time and priorities.

## Step 5: Practice self-compassion

Saying "no" can be challenging, especially if you're worried about disappointing others. Remind yourself that it's okay to prioritize your goals and well-being, and that setting boundaries is essential for long-term success.

Consider these thought-provoking questions as you work on mastering the art of saying "no":

- How can I improve my ability to assess opportunities and requests objectively?
- What strategies can I use to say "no" assertively and respectfully?
- How can I better manage my feelings of guilt or fear when saying "no" to others?

In the next chapter, we will discuss mindfulness and time management, focusing on how to enhance your concentration and reduce stress for greater success. By mastering the art of saying "no," you can protect your time, maintain your focus, and ultimately achieve your entrepreneurial goals.

# Chapter 19 - Mindfulness and Time Management: Enhancing Focus and Reducing Stress for Greater Success

In today's fast-paced world, entrepreneurs often face numerous demands and distractions. Mindfulness, the practice of being present and fully engaged with our experiences, can help you better manage your time and reduce stress. In this chapter, we will explore how mindfulness can enhance your focus and improve your overall time management skills.

**Step 1: Understand the principles of mindfulness**

Mindfulness is about being fully present in the moment, without judgment or distraction. It involves paying attention to your thoughts, feelings, and experiences as they arise, allowing you to respond more effectively to the demands of your day.

**Step 2: Develop a mindfulness practice**

To cultivate mindfulness, consider incorporating meditation or other mindfulness techniques into your daily routine. Start with a few minutes each day and gradually increase the duration as you become more comfortable. Here are some mindfulness exercises to try:

- Breath awareness: Focus on the sensation of your breath as you inhale and exhale.
- Body scan: Bring awareness to each part of your body, noting any sensations or tension.
- Loving-kindness meditation: Cultivate feelings of compassion and love for yourself and others.

**Step 3: Apply mindfulness to your daily activities**

As you become more familiar with mindfulness practices, work on incorporating them into your daily activities. This might involve:

- Taking short mindfulness breaks throughout the day to refocus and recharge.
- Practicing mindful listening during meetings and conversations.
- Using mindfulness to help you prioritize tasks and make more intentional decisions.

## Step 4: Monitor your progress and adjust as needed

As with any new skill, it's essential to assess your progress and make adjustments as needed. Reflect on how mindfulness has impacted your focus, productivity, and stress levels, and consider making changes to your practice to better support your goals.

Consider these thought-provoking questions as you integrate mindfulness into your time management approach:

- How does mindfulness influence my ability to prioritize tasks and make decisions?
- In what areas of my life can I apply mindfulness to improve my focus and reduce stress?
- How can I maintain my mindfulness practice in the face of challenges and setbacks?

In the next chapter, we will explore time management case studies, examining the lessons learned from successful entrepreneurs who mastered the clock. By incorporating mindfulness into your time management strategy, you can enhance your focus, reduce stress, and ultimately achieve greater success in your entrepreneurial journey.

# Chapter 20 - Time Management Case Studies: Lessons from Successful Entrepreneurs Who Mastered the Clock

In this chapter, we will examine several case studies of successful entrepreneurs who have mastered the art of time management. By learning from their experiences and strategies, you can apply these valuable lessons to your own entrepreneurial journey.

**Case Study 1: Elon Musk - Time Blocking**

Elon Musk, the visionary entrepreneur behind Tesla, SpaceX, and Neuralink, is known for his impressive productivity. One of his key time management strategies is time blocking, which involves scheduling tasks in focused blocks of time. This allows him to allocate his energy and attention effectively, ensuring that he can accomplish his ambitious goals.

Questions to consider:

- How can I implement time blocking in my own schedule to maximize productivity?

- What tasks should I prioritize during my most focused time blocks?

**Case Study 2: Arianna Huffington - The Importance of Sleep and Rest**

Arianna Huffington, the co-founder of The Huffington Post, experienced a wake-up call when she collapsed from exhaustion. This led her to recognize the importance of rest and sleep in her daily routine. By prioritizing her well-being and setting boundaries around her work, she was able to boost her productivity and achieve greater success.

Questions to consider:

- How can I prioritize rest and self-care in my own schedule?
- What boundaries can I set to protect my time and energy?

## Case Study 3: Tim Ferriss - The 80/20 Rule

Best-selling author and entrepreneur Tim Ferriss is an advocate for the 80/20 rule, also known as the Pareto Principle. This principle states that 80% of your results come from 20% of your efforts. By identifying and focusing on high-impact tasks, Ferriss has been able to achieve remarkable success with minimal effort.

Questions to consider:

- How can I apply the 80/20 rule to my own business?
- What tasks generate the most significant results with the least amount of effort?

## Case Study 4: Sheryl Sandberg - Prioritization and Goal Setting

Sheryl Sandberg, the COO of Facebook and author of "Lean In," emphasizes the importance of prioritization and goal setting. By clearly defining her goals and focusing on her top priorities, she can effectively manage her time and achieve her objectives.

Questions to consider:

- How can I set clear goals and priorities for my business?
- How can I ensure that I am consistently working towards my most important objectives?

As you reflect on these case studies, consider how you can apply the lessons learned to your own time management strategies. By integrating these proven techniques into your daily routine, you will be well on your way to clocking your way to triumph and unlocking the time management secrets of successful entrepreneurs. In the upcoming chapters, we will delve deeper into more time management strategies to help you on your path to success.

# Thank You

Dear Valued Reader,

From the depths of my heart, I would like to extend a monumental and sincere thank you for choosing to embark on this transformative journey by reading "Clocking Your Way to Triumph: Unlock the Time Management Secrets of Successful Entrepreneurs." Your decision to invest your precious time in this book reflects your unyielding commitment to personal growth and entrepreneurial excellence.

You have taken a courageous step by choosing to unlock the potential that lies within you, and I am deeply honored to have been a part of this empowering expedition. Together, we have explored the hidden pathways to success, learned from the wisdom of accomplished entrepreneurs, and discovered the secrets that will propel you to new heights in your business endeavors.

As you turn the final page, remember that this is not the end but rather the beginning of a thrilling new chapter in your life. The knowledge, strategies, and insights you have gained will serve as the catalyst that sparks a fire within you, igniting an unrelenting drive for accomplishment and self-mastery.

I urge you to continue harnessing the power of time management, honing your focus, and prioritizing your goals. The world awaits your brilliance, and the only limits you face are the ones you set for yourself. Always remember that success is not a destination but a continuous journey, and the time has come for you to forge your path and write your own story.

Stay inspired, stay motivated, and never forget that the most powerful force you possess is the belief in yourself and your ability to overcome all obstacles. Time is the canvas upon which you will paint the masterpiece of your life, and I have no doubt that your future will be a breathtaking work of art.

Once again, thank you for allowing me to be a part of your journey. May you continue to rise, conquer, and clock your way to triumph!

With unyielding gratitude and admiration,

Aditya